# BRAIN BOOSTERS

# UNDER THE SEA PUZZLES

by
Vicky Barker
& Ste Johnson

**LiTtle**
GENIUS
**BOOks**

Published by Little Genius Books. www.littlegeniusbooks.com. • 10 9 8 7 6 5 4 3 2 1 • 9781953344632

Text and illustrations copyright © 2021 b small publishing ltd. Art Director: Vicky Barker. Editorial: Sam Hutchinson. Printed in China by WKT Co. Ltd.

Add sad faces or happy faces to these seahorses.
Draw patterns on them and color them in.

# Follow the path to find out where these whales are heading.

C A T I R C T A N A

## DID YOU KNOW?

Humpback whales migrate to warmer waters in winter to have their babies before travelling back to colder regions to feed.

Dave only makes bubbles with even answers.
Marina only makes the ones with odd answers.
Which dolphin makes the most bubbles?

Dave

3 x 9

2 + 4

11 − 5

5 x 5

13 + 7

12 − 8

20 − 6

7 x 4

6 x 5

28 ÷ 7

19 − 10

9 x 7

6 x 3

3 x 8

36 − 6

16 − 9

Marina

How many complete scuba suits can you put together with these items below?

**DID YOU KNOW?**

Scuba stands for Self-contained Underwater Breathing Apparatus.

# Join the dots to see who is visiting this coral reef. Color in the beautiful scene.

# Which explorer finds the deep-sea creature first?
Work out the sums. The submarine with the highest total wins!
Use a separate piece of paper if you need to.

A

B

C

24 ÷ 4

21 ÷ 3

5 - 4

3 × 9

9 + 6

15 ÷ 5

14 - 8

8 + 8

12 - 4

**DID YOU KNOW?**

6 × 4

4 × 3

18 + 6

The deepest ocean
trench found so far
is the Mariana Trench.
Explorers have measured
as far as 36,201 feet
(11,034 m) deep.

Help this fish choose the safest
route back to their home.

Starting at "WHALE" and without taking your pen off the page, follow the letters around until you have found each of the eight types of shark in this grid.

START HERE →

```
W H A L E B A S K I
L U B R E G I T O N
L G R E A T W H K G
E S R U N E T I A M
H A M M E R H E A D
```

### DID YOU KNOW?

*Greenland sharks are the longest-living vertebrate species on the planet. One study found that they can live for over 500 years!*

Take a dip into this underwater word search.

| F | Y | Y | D | I | V | E | R | V | M | S | H | H | S | H | L |
|---|---|---|---|---|---|---|---|---|---|---|---|---|---|---|---|
| I | A | N | E | M | O | N | E | P | E | U | S | X | T | M | O |
| H | S | Q | S | P | E | C | I | A | S | I | L | U | U | E | B |
| S | T | O | U | S | H | E | L | L | S | D | A | S | N | X | S |
| I | A | W | R | I | C | O | R | A | L | E | A | I | T | M | T |
| F | P | F | H | V | D | E | B | L | S | A | R | A | L | J | E |
| Y | F | E | F | A | S | L | E | P | H | A | H | W | E | H | R |
| L | H | H | F | X | L | L | E | A | M | S | H | A | R | K | D |
| L | S | S | B | E | G | E | X | B | O | C | X | S | V | H | L |
| E | H | I | H | S | D | F | U | C | R | T | T | E | H | O | B |
| J | S | F | L | O | W | S | N | K | L | O | U | A | W | C | A |
| B | H | N | A | R | W | H | A | L | X | P | R | W | U | T | R |
| Q | R | G | X | J | F | O | C | E | A | N | T | E | L | O | C |
| G | I | O | C | B | A | N | S | H | E | S | L | E | E | P | M |
| J | M | L | S | E | A | H | O | R | S | E | E | D | H | U | P |
| K | P | A | H | E | E | K | S | D | A | X | M | V | A | S | C |

| WHALE | CRAB | CORAL | DEEP SEA |
|---|---|---|---|
| NARWHAL | SEAWEED | JELLYFISH | SHRIMP |
| SEAL | DIVER | SHELLS | ANEMONE |
| SHARK | SUBMARINE | LOBSTER | FISH |
| OCEAN | SEAHORSE | OCTOPUS | TURTLE |

Each of these sets of bubbles has a different number pattern. Can you work out the pattern and fill in the blank spaces?

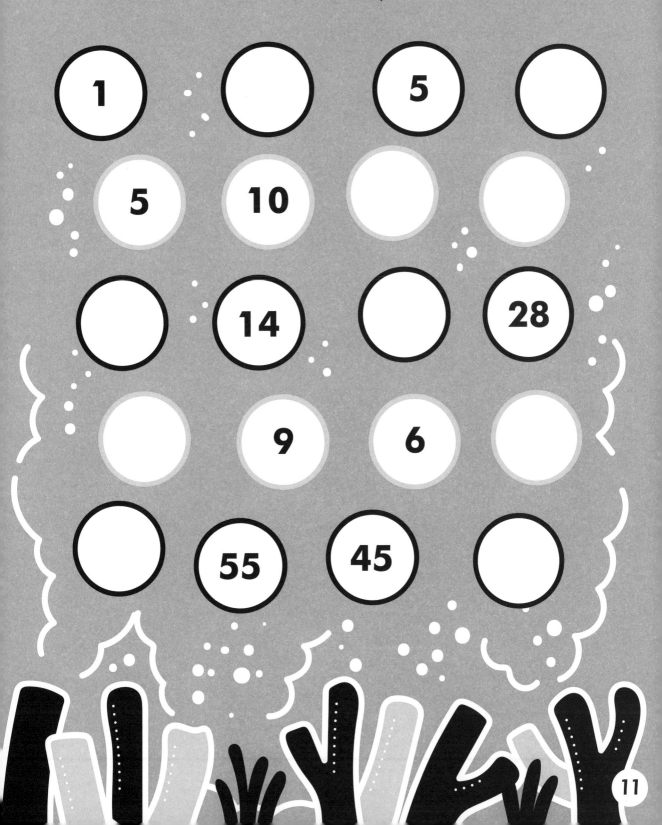

# Find the odd one out in each row.

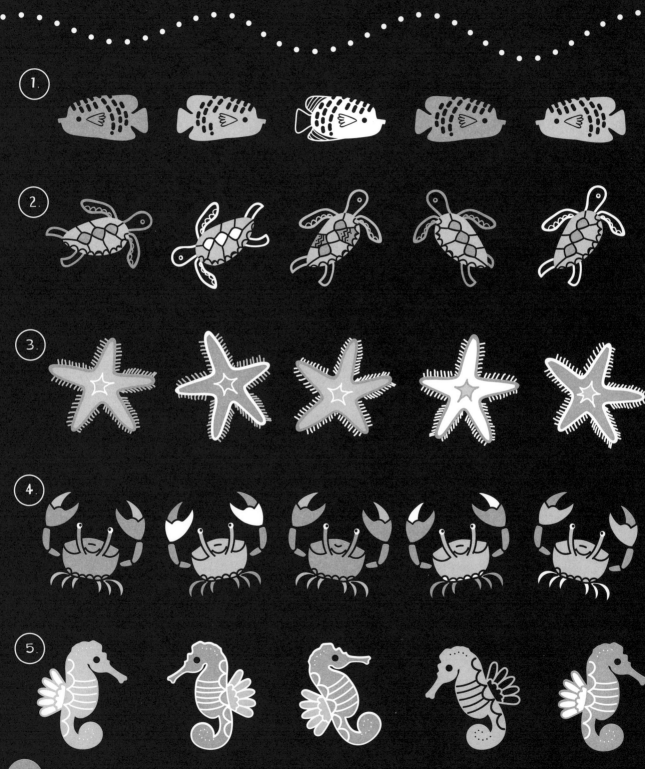

# Match these sea creatures to their shadows.

You are off on your sea exploration!
What can you see?

# True or false?

**1.** A group of jellyfish is called a smack.

**2.** Crabs can only walk sideways.

**3.** A dolphin is a very big fish.

**4.** A sea anemone's mouth also serves as its bottom.

**5.** Whales have belly buttons.

**6.** Scientists have discovered a new species in the North Sea called a bone-eating snot flower.

## Sub Team, Captain's Log:

*My team finally arrived at the shipwreck
we have spent months searching for.
After a careful approach, we were faced
with something we never could have imagined.*

_____

_____

_____

_____

_____

_____

_____

_____

# Can you spot ten differences in these scenes?

**DID YOU KNOW?**

*Pinniped is the scientific name for any type of seal. It means fin-footed in Latin. Those fin-shaped feet make them amazing swimmers.*

# Help this explorer find the lost underwater city. Watch out for the sharks!

Use this step-by-step guide to draw a cute narwhal.

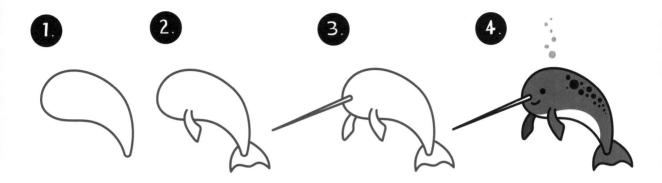

1.

2.

3.

4.

## DID YOU KNOW?

*Narwhals are sometimes called the unicorns of the sea.
The males have a long tusk (which is actually a tooth) that
can grow up to 10 feet (3 m) long!*

Find the group of sea creatures that matches the one on the right.

20

You have discovered a new species of deep-sea creature! Draw what it looks like and give it a name.

There are some deep-sea species with brilliant names such as the Christmas tree worm, nudibranch, sea angel, red-lipped batfish, coffinfish, blobfish (aka fathead) and yeti crab. Can you find out more about these amazing creatures?

21

Help these divers on their quest to find treasure on this shipwreck. Watch out for dangers blocking your path!.

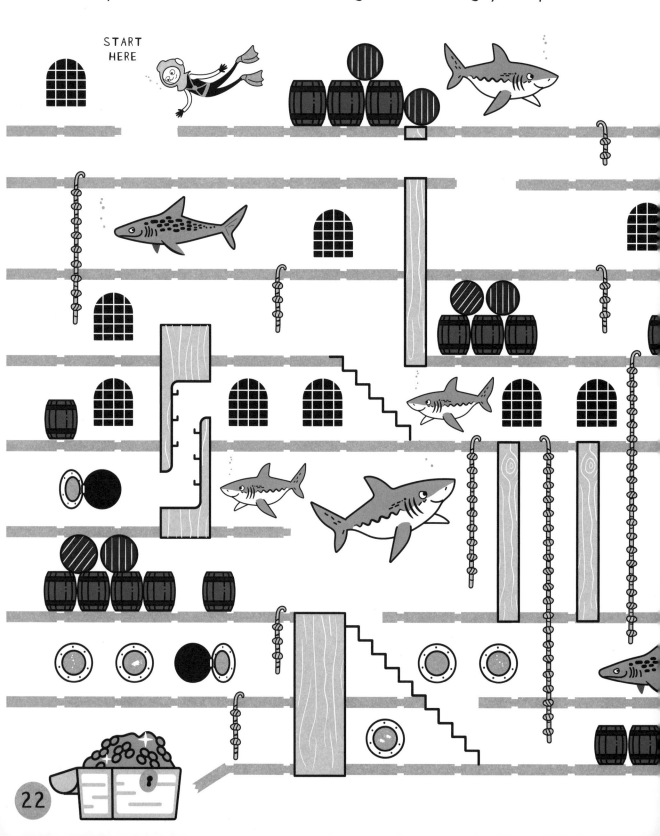

Draw the rest of these
cephalopods and color them in.

How quickly can you get this sailfish from A to B?
Draw a line as fast as you can without going off the sides.
Time yourself!

**DID YOU KNOW?**

With top speeds of 70 miles (113 km) per hour, the sailfish is widely considered the fastest fish in the ocean!

# Can you copy this ray picture in the grid below?

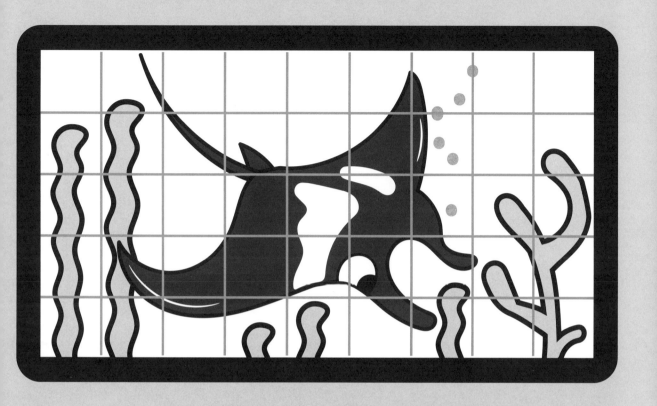

Follow the seaweed path to help this
sea otter back to the surface.

Subtract all the spaces with a dot marked in them by coloring them in. You will reveal a picture in the space left behind!

# Are these crabs or shells?

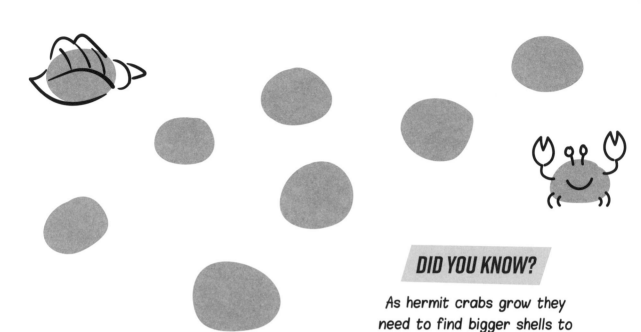

## DID YOU KNOW?

As hermit crabs grow they need to find bigger shells to shelter their soft bodies.

Can you work out the answers to these?

$$\text{🐚} + \text{🐚} + \text{🐚} = 9$$

$$\text{🐚} + \text{🐚} + \text{🐚} = 18$$

# Or maybe you prefer tentacles? You decide!

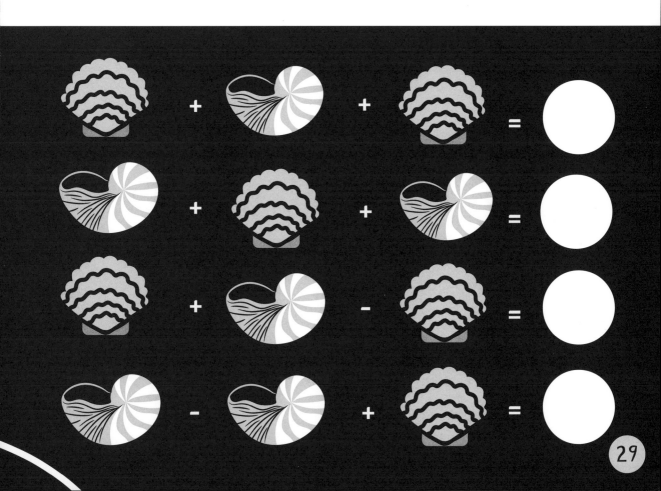

One of these scuba suits is unique.
Can you spot which one?

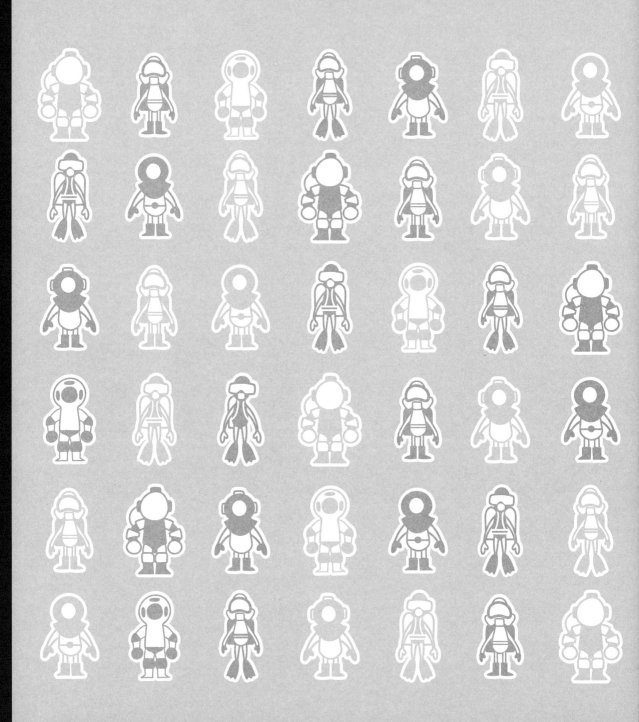

# Are there more blue bubbles or grey shrimp?

## DID YOU KNOW?

Shrimp are grey in color but turn pink when we cook them to eat!

*gulp!*

What is out of place
in this scene?

32

Can you work out the pattern that these starfish follow?
Fill in the missing shapes with the right pattern.

# Is there an odd or even number of seahorses below?
## Count them and find out!

# Can you spot ten differences in these scenes?

**DID YOU KNOW?** It is estimated that there are over 3 million shipwrecks worldwide. Some have been there for thousands of years.

35

# Can you find the row that matches the silhouettes?

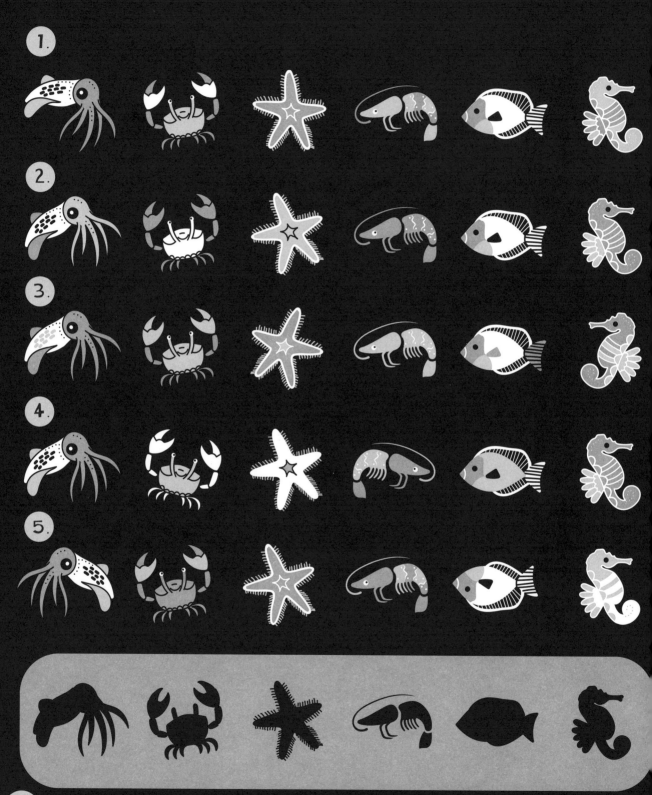

# Fishing time! Who's catching what?

Add legs to the jellyfish so that each row
(across, down and diagonal) adds up to 15.

Can you complete this picture grid? Fill in all of the boxes with one of the four pictures. Every column, row and four-square block must contain one of each.

## QUICK QUIZ!

**1.** Seahorses are the only animals ...

    a) that look like a horse.    b) where the male gives birth.

    c) that really dislike their name.    d) that can play the trumpet.

**2.** A shrimp's heart is ...

    a) big and full of love.    b) in its head.

    c) in its tail.    d) in its bottom.

**3.** Dolphins sleep ...

    a) with one eye open.    b) far too much.

    c) to get out of doing work.    d) for ten hours a day.

**4.** A starfish has no ...

    a) heart.    b) stomach.

    c) worries.    d) style.

**5.** One quarter of marine life live ...

    a) in caravans.    b) under the sand.

    c) in coral reefs.    d) underwater.

Only two of these fish are identical.
Can you spot which two?

Does Dougie the dugong or Martha the manatee reach the tastiest leaves at the top first? Solve the sums and the one with the highest score wins!

7 + 16

5 + 13

23 – 8

17 – 9

6 x 4

9 x 3

15 + 6

14 + 3

35 ÷ 7

7 x 5

11 x 4

24 ÷ 6

Dougie

Martha

42

# Can you find these squares in the picture below?

Can you break this code to reveal the picture?
Color in each of the squares in this list to see what is hidden.

A - 9, 10
B - 10
C - 10
D - 10
E - 8, 9, 10, 11, 12
F - 8, 12
G - 8, 12
H - 8, 12
I - 8, 12
J - 6, 7, 13, 14

K - 4, 5, 6, 10, 11,
      14, 15, 16
L - 3, 6, 9, 12, 14, 17
M - 2, 6, 8, 13, 14, 18
N - 2, 6, 9, 12, 14, 18
O - 3, 6, 10, 11, 14, 17
P - 4, 5, 6, 14, 15, 16
Q - 6, 7, 13, 14
R - 8, 9, 10, 11, 12

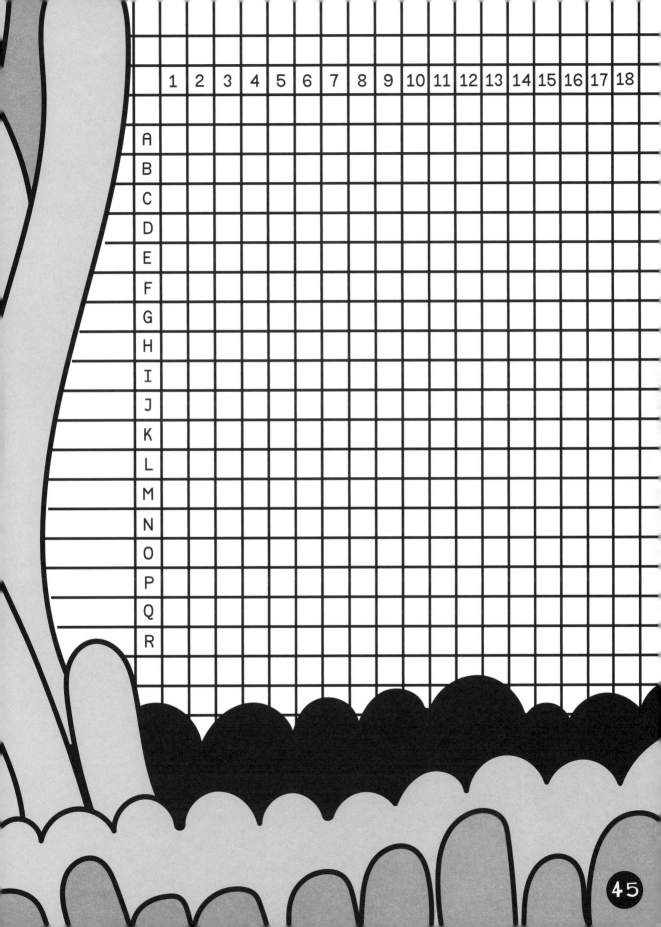

|   | 1 | 2 | 3 | 4 | 5 | 6 | 7 | 8 | 9 | 10 | 11 | 12 | 13 | 14 | 15 | 16 | 17 | 18 |
|---|---|---|---|---|---|---|---|---|---|----|----|----|----|----|----|----|----|----|
| A |   |   |   |   |   |   |   |   |   |    |    |    |    |    |    |    |    |    |
| B |   |   |   |   |   |   |   |   |   |    |    |    |    |    |    |    |    |    |
| C |   |   |   |   |   |   |   |   |   |    |    |    |    |    |    |    |    |    |
| D |   |   |   |   |   |   |   |   |   |    |    |    |    |    |    |    |    |    |
| E |   |   |   |   |   |   |   |   |   |    |    |    |    |    |    |    |    |    |
| F |   |   |   |   |   |   |   |   |   |    |    |    |    |    |    |    |    |    |
| G |   |   |   |   |   |   |   |   |   |    |    |    |    |    |    |    |    |    |
| H |   |   |   |   |   |   |   |   |   |    |    |    |    |    |    |    |    |    |
| I |   |   |   |   |   |   |   |   |   |    |    |    |    |    |    |    |    |    |
| J |   |   |   |   |   |   |   |   |   |    |    |    |    |    |    |    |    |    |
| K |   |   |   |   |   |   |   |   |   |    |    |    |    |    |    |    |    |    |
| L |   |   |   |   |   |   |   |   |   |    |    |    |    |    |    |    |    |    |
| M |   |   |   |   |   |   |   |   |   |    |    |    |    |    |    |    |    |    |
| N |   |   |   |   |   |   |   |   |   |    |    |    |    |    |    |    |    |    |
| O |   |   |   |   |   |   |   |   |   |    |    |    |    |    |    |    |    |    |
| P |   |   |   |   |   |   |   |   |   |    |    |    |    |    |    |    |    |    |
| Q |   |   |   |   |   |   |   |   |   |    |    |    |    |    |    |    |    |    |
| R |   |   |   |   |   |   |   |   |   |    |    |    |    |    |    |    |    |    |

# Answers

## Page 3
**ANTARCTICA**

## Page 4
EVEN = 11
ODD = 5
Dave wins!

## Page 5

You can make five complete scuba suits.

## Page 6

## Page 7
A = 32    B = 65    C = 52

B reaches the creature first.

## Page 8

## Page 9
WHALEBASKI
LUBREGITON
LGREATWHKG
ESRUNETIAM
HAMMERHEAD

## Page 10

## Page 11

## Page 12
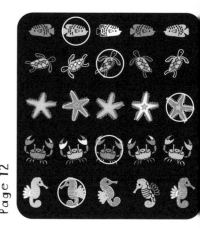

## Page 13
(image)

## Page 15
1. True      4. True
2. False     5. True
3. False     6. True

How did you do?

46

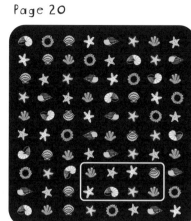

Page 22

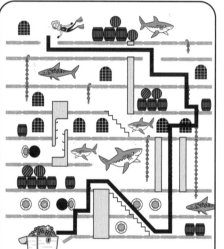

Page 26

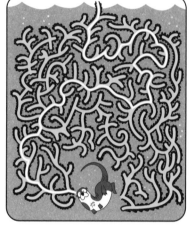

Page 27

Page 29

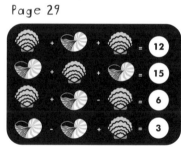

Page 30

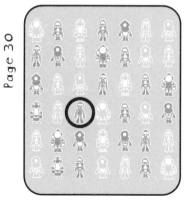

Page 31 – There are more shrimp.

Page 32

Page 33

Page 34    EVEN   There are 16 seahorses.

47

## Page 35

## Page 36 – Row 2

## Page 37

1. C    2. A    3. B

## Page 38

## Page 39

## Page 41

## Page 40

1. b
2. b
3. a
4. a
5. c

## Page 42

D = 120

M = 121

Martha reaches the top first.

## Page 43

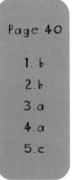

## Pages 44-45